The Sugar Maple

The Sugar Maple

by

Rosamond S. Metcalf

with photographs by

James Hearne

PHOENIX PUBLISHING

Canaan, New Hampshire

Metcalf, Rosamond S.
    The sugar maple.

        Summary: Uses the activities of a classroom of chil-
dren to introduce sugar maples and syrup making.
        1. Sugar-maple—Juvenile literature.   2. Maple syrup
—Juvenile literature. [1. Maple syrup]   I. Hearne, James,
ill.   II. Title.
SB239.M3M47   664'.132   82-595
ISBN 0-914016-87-3   AACR2

Printed in the United States of America
by Courier Printing Company
Design by A.L. Morris

Acknowledgments

WE WISH TO THANK the Acworth Five-Point Dandys, the Charlestown Hemlock Hi-Toppers, and the South Charlestown Jim Dandies 4-H Clubs for supplying the students for Mrs. Edwards's class. We also thank the following sugar houses for permitting photographs to be taken of the sugaring process:

Kenneth and Ruth Bascom
Bascom's Sugar House
Alstead, NH

Alvin and Nancy Clark
Clark Sugar House
Alstead, NH

Wayne Deabill
Four Seasons Sugar House
Charlestown, NH

Putnam Brothers
Putnam's Sugar House
Charlestown, NH

George Titus
Hemlock Road
Charlestown, NH

A special thank you goes to Marion Bascom, who played the part of Mrs. Edwards, to Ernest and Howard Hill of Charlestown whose photographs appear as a frontispiece on page ii, and to all who encouraged us to proceed with the book.

Rosamond Metcalf
James Hearne

The Sugar Maple

One day Mrs. Edwards took her class for a walk. They were looking for acorns, leaves, and grasses for an October art project.

There was a large tree in front of Jennifer's house. "That's a sugar maple," Mrs. Edwards told her students.

"I like the pretty red and yellow leaves," Laurie said.

Kevin picked up a few and put them in his bag. "Why do they call it a *sugar* maple?" he asked.

"Does anyone know?" Mrs. Edwards looked about her. Danny and Laurie had the answer, but no one else knew, not even Billy.

"That's a sugar maple."

Then Mrs. Edwards had an idea. "I'm going to talk to Jennifer's mother. Maybe she will let us adopt this tree. Then we can learn all about it."

During the next few weeks the children made several visits to the tree. They decided to give it a name.

"Let's call it Mr. Sweet," David suggested. "If it's a *sugar* maple it must be *sweet.*"

"It probably grows sugar cubes," laughed Billy.

Mrs. Edwards smiled. "David may be smarter than you think!"

Each day the class visited Mr. Sweet they noticed something different. They watched the leaves turn from red and yellow to rust. They saw a strong wind knock them off the tree. Then they found some winged seeds left there since spring. Danny measured one; it was about an inch long.

"That's two and a half centimeters," said Billy.

They guessed at the height of the tree. "It's *very* tall," Jennifer observed. "It's taller than my house!"

"It's at least fifty feet high," Mrs. Edwards guessed. "This tree has been around a long time."

"Fifteen meters," said Billy.

"Just about an inch long."

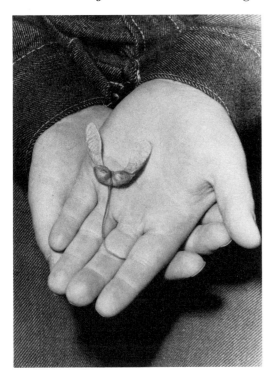

"Look again at Mr. Sweet." Mrs. Edwards pointed to the tree. "What do you see that makes this tree different from other trees?"

"The branches are smooth, but the trunk is rough," Debbie replied.

"Its top is fat in the middle—the top of the tree is shaped like an egg," Laurie added.

"That's oval-shaped," explained Billy.

"And the color," David pointed out, "is gray on the branches but the trunk is darker."

"Good," Mrs. Edwards said. "Now you're using your eyes."

A few more weeks went by and the children became busy with other things. They decorated the classroom with red and green paper chains. They made Santa faces with cotton beards. Soon it was vacation time, with snow and ice for sliding and skating. On Valentine's Day the boys and girls glued pink and red hearts onto white paper doilies. They had forgotten Mr. Sweet.

One day toward the end of February Mrs. Edwards mentioned the maple tree again. "It's time to find out more about Mr. Sweet," she said. "What is a sugar maple? Why is it important to us? Danny's father and mother have invited us to visit their sugar house, but we need to do some research first. Go to the library. Use the encyclopedia. Ask your parents. Find out everything you can!"

The next day the children told what they had learned. Debbie said, "I can write the Latin name for sugar maple. It's in my father's botany book." Carefully she wrote the words *Acer saccharum* on the chalkboard.

"Can you pronounce it?" Billy asked.

"Well . . ." Debbie hesitated.

Danny interrupted. "My father told me some other names for the sugar maple. Sometimes it's called a hard maple or a rock maple."

*"I can spell it,
but I'm not sure how to pronounce it."*

"I looked in a tree book to find out where it grows," David said. "It's one of about twelve maples that grow wild in the United States and Canada. It's found in the northern states."

Jennifer raised her hand and Mrs. Edwards nodded at her. "I learned that its hard wood is used for furniture, cabinets, and flooring," she said. "Some people think it makes excellent canoe paddles. The early colonists used the ashes in soapmaking."

Billy laughed. "I'd use it for firewood."

"I didn't know there are so many different kinds of maples!"

"You haven't told me its most important use," Mrs. Edwards said.

"Maple syrup!" the children shouted all together.

Kevin explained that maple syrup is made in all the New England states as well as in New York, Ohio, Michigan, Pennsylvania, Wisconsin, Minnesota, West Virginia, and Maryland. "My dad grew up in Quebec, and he told me that large amounts of syrup are made in Canada, too. He also said it is sold all over the United States and in many other countries."

"Right!" Mrs. Edwards agreed. "More than two-thirds of the world's syrup is made in Quebec. But do you know *how* it's made?"

"Maple syrup is made in all the New England states."

"I do," Laurie said. "You drill holes into the tree trunk and then hammer a tap, or spigot, into each of the holes. When the sap starts to rise we tap some trees in back of our house. Then we make buckets out of empty bleach bottles and hang them on the taps. My brother and I collect the sap and pour it into a large plastic barrel where we store it. My dad built a big pan which he sets up on bricks, and when the barrel is full, we boil off the water. We do most of the boiling outdoors. Then my mom finishes it on the kitchen stove. When most of the water is boiled off, we are left with delicious sweet syrup."

"When pussy willows blossom, sugaring is at its best."

Then Mrs. Edwards asked, "Do you know how much sap it takes to make a gallon of syrup?"

"We make five or six quarts of syrup every year," Laurie replied. "I don't know how much sap we use, but it seems like a lot. It takes almost all day to boil it down."

"It takes 151 liters to make four liters of syrup," said Billy. "That's 40 gallons of sap to make a gallon."

"What did Laurie mean when she said they tap when the sap is rising?" Mrs. Edwards asked.

"Well," David explained, "in late winter when the buds and grasses are beginning to wake up, but it's not time yet for them to start growing, the sap starts to rise."

"That's when we begin sugaring," Danny agreed. "The sap runs best when the days are warm but the nights are still cold. After about a month it gets too warm and the sap isn't good any more."

"The sap is best when the pussy willows are blossoming," Laurie told the class. "When we hear the first frog peepers, we know the sap run is almost over."

"Doesn't it hurt the trees when you put holes in them?" Debbie asked.

"Let's save that question for Danny's mother," Mrs. Edwards suggested. "We're going to the sugar house tomorrow."

10   The next morning the children climbed into a big yellow school bus which drove through town and out into the country. They passed farms and fields. Soon the bus was bumping through the woods along a muddy road. Outside they saw long lines of colored plastic tubing, crisscrossing from tree to tree like a city highway and leading finally to large holding tanks placed along the side of the road. At one tank a tractor was parked. Some men were pumping the sap into a tank on the back of the tractor with a gasoline powered pump.

"Where are the buckets?" Kevin asked.

Danny explained, "It's much faster and easier to collect the sap this way. Gravity keeps it flowing down to the tanks. By pumping the sap out of the tanks, we don't have to carry each bucket one at a time. We use buckets only in flat places where gravity won't work."

"*Gravity,*" said Billy, "is what makes an apple fall on your head."

"Tubing is faster and easier."

"*But where tubing
won't work buckets are used.*"

"I see bubbles!"

Finally the bus turned into a driveway. A sign in front read "White's Sugar House." Mrs. White was waiting there for them.

She took the children along a path where they could see the plastic tubing close up. "I see bubbles moving inside!" David cried.

"The sap is moving down toward the holding tank," Mrs. White explained.

She showed them some old-fashioned wooden buckets. The children peered inside. "Looks like water to me," said Billy.

"Looks like water to me."

14

"Taste it," Mrs. White suggested.

One by one the children dipped their fingers into the bucket and licked them. "It's like sweet water," Kevin said.

"Try this!" Laurie smiled as she lifted the bucket off the spigot and bent down to drink straight from the tap.

"The Indians taught the early colonists how to make syrup," Mrs. White explained. "The colonists tapped the . . ."

"Who taught the Indians?" Billy interrupted.

"Take the bucket off to get a taste."   *"Even teacher tries it."*

"This bucket is almost full!"

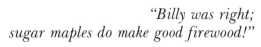

"Billy was right;
sugar maples do make good firewood!"

"We don't know," Mrs. White continued. "Some people believe that a lazy squaw made the discovery when she went down to the river for water one day. She passed by a tree where a clear liquid was dripping out of a woodpecker hole. 'Aha,' she thought. 'I'll get my water here and I won't have to walk so far.' She set the pot on the fire to boil and put some venison into it. When the Indian brave tasted his dinner he decided his squaw was the best cook in the village. He liked the taste of his venison cooked with this strange thick syrup."

"The early settlers tapped the trees with an axe, making huge gashes which killed many of them," Mrs. White went on. "The sap was caught in troughs cut out of logs and it was boiled down in kettles hung over a big fire. This was a messy way to make syrup. Come inside, and you'll see that we've made many improvements over the years."

The children turned toward the sugar house. Steam was billowing around the roof and there was a sweet smell in the air.

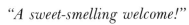

"A sweet-smelling welcome!"

Inside, the sweet smell was even stronger. There was a woodsy smell, too. The children blinked as they entered the large, dark room. Drops of water on the panes made it hard to see out the tiny window. "It smells like the pancakes we ate when we went camping last summer," David said.

They gathered around a large, flat, open pan. Kevin put his hands near it to warm them. "Is it going to boil over?" he asked. Clouds of steam rolled around him.

Mrs. White laughed. "No, it won't boil over. This is called an *evaporator*. A fire underneath keeps the sap boiling at just the right temperature. And it won't burn because we keep adding more sap as it boils down. The steam around you is the water that we are boiling away. The heavier syrup works its way through those channels in the pan until it's ready to be drawn off. Then we strain it through a felt and pour it into cans, bottles, or plastic containers." She held up several sizes of plastic jugs.

*"We'll help you
sell your maple products, Mrs. White."*

"*Grandpa stokes the fire.*"

*"This sap yoke is heavy.
I like plastic tubing much better!"*

24

"The colors are different."

"What is Mr. White doing?" Debbie asked. Mr. White was studying a set of glass bottles in a rack.

"I'm checking the grade," he replied. "We grade our syrup by its color. There are three Grade A table syrups, called light amber, medium amber, and dark amber. Some people prefer the darker syrup because it has a stronger flavor. The darkest, Grade B, is sold to companies which make pancake syrup from mixtures of cane sugar and maple syrup."

"How do you make maple sugar candy?" Jennifer wanted to know.

"Maple cream, sugar candy, and sugar-on-snow are made from maple syrup that is boiled down a little longer. With a candy thermometer, your mom can make these in her kitchen. The candy comes out especially pretty when you use a mold," Mrs. White replied.

"The early settlers made sugar candy bricks. For many children, it was the only sweetening they knew. They would chip off a piece to suck on or to add to their tea," Mrs. White added.

The children asked more questions. Then they saw the pipes leading from the holding tanks outside to the evaporator pans inside the building. They learned that producers use oil, gas, or wood to fire their evaporator pans. Debbie asked whether tapping hurts the trees.

"Do your mom and dad give blood when the Bloodmobile comes to town?" Mrs. White asked. Debbie nodded. "Well, tapping a tree is like giving blood. Only grownups are asked to give blood. A tree is big enough to start tapping when it's about forty years old. We are careful to limit the number of taps we place in each tree, and we find that a healthy tree recovers quickly. Most tap holes give about ten to fifteen gallons of sap each year without causing harm."

"That's about 38 to 57 liters," said Billy.

"Actually," Mrs. White added, "one of the greatest dangers to sugar maples is road salt."

"Oh yes," Laurie agreed, "my dad worries about the trees that grow near the road by our house. The town trucks spread salt on icy roads, and the salt soaks down to the roots. Some of our trees are dying."

"Yum . . . this is good!"

When all questions were answered, Mrs. White brought out some pans filled with snow. The children sat down at picnic tables while she dribbled over the snow a thick syrup that had been cooked to the candy stage. It hardened quickly into a sticky mass. The children dipped forks into it, brought up chunks, and tasted the delicious sugar-on-snow. "Yum," they murmured, licking their lips. Mrs. White then gave them sour pickles to take away the sweetness, and they were ready for seconds.

"Back to the bus, boys and girls."

28

Before long it was time to board the bus. "Thank you, Mrs. White," the children shouted.

"Where's Billy?" David asked.

Mrs. Edwards went back to find him. He was talking to Grandpa White about the cost of operating the evaporators.

"It's very expensive," Grandpa said. "When the sap run is good, we boil day and night. It takes a lot of fuel. We're thinking of putting in a reverse osmosis machine. It's a large machine that will take off three-fourths of the water before we boil."

Billy nodded. "That would save you a lot of fuel because you wouldn't have to boil so long."

*"These evaporators
are expensive to operate."*

"Come, Billy," Mrs. Edwards called.

The children looked longingly out the window as the bus drove slowly down the lane. It had been a wonderful visit.

Back at school the boys and girls drew pictures and wrote stories about their trip. They wrote thank-you letters to Mr. and Mrs. White.

When they finished Mrs. Edwards said that tomorrow they would drill a hole in Mr. Sweet's tree trunk and place a tap in it. If they could collect enough sap, they would boil it down on a hot plate in the classroom. Then they would have a taste of their own sugar-on-snow.

"Now do you agree that Mr. Sweet is a good name for our tree?" Mrs. Edwards asked. Everyone nodded except Billy, who thought "Yum-Yum" would have been better.

The children looked back longingly.

p. 4 sugar house This is a building in which the sugaring equipment is stored. It is opened up during the sugaring season (February-April) and the syrup is made here. It is large enough to hold one or two evaporators, one or more picnic tables (for visitors who are always welcome), a sales area where maple products are displayed, and the woodpile (if wood is used for fuel). It has vents in the roof where steam can escape.

p. 4 botany book A botany book is a book about plant life.

p. 8 tap, spigot A tap or spigot is a small spout that is hammered into a hole in the tree. It can be made of metal or plastic (old-fashioned ones were carved out of wood) and it extends one to two inches (3-4 cm) into the tree. The sap drips through it into the bucket or tubing. To "tap" a tree is to drill the hole and then place the spigot into it. Some producers do their tapping in mid-winter, long before the sap rises. Then they are ready to boil as soon as the sap flows.

p. 8 sap Sap is the liquid that circulates through a plant, carrying water and food as blood does in animals.

p. 9 sugaring Sugaring is the process of making maple syrup. It includes tapping, collecting, boiling, and bottling.

p. 9 peepers Peepers are tree frogs. They are about one and a half inches long (about 4 cm) and are brown in color. They are almost never seen; but the chirping

sound of the males, calling to their mates, is a welcome sign of spring. They can be heard in every pond or marsh soon after the ice melts.

p. 10 holding tank A holding tank is usually a large metal tank, shaped like a bathtub, into which the sap drips from the tubing. Large drums or other containers are also used.

p. 10 gravity Gravity is the natural force that causes objects to move down toward the center of the earth. Billy is referring to the story of Isaac Newton, who discovered gravity when an apple fell on his head.

p. 18 trough A trough is an open basin, often carved out of wood.

p. 20 evaporator The large flat pans in which sap is boiled are called evaporators.

p. 20 felt A felt is a piece of cloth which strains out bits of dirt and bark.

p. 24 amber Amber is a color, reddish-yellow.

p. 25 sugar-on-snow Maple syrup that is boiled to a temperature of 22° to 25° above the boiling point of water (212°) makes tasty sugar-on-snow.

p. 25 maple cream Maple syrup boiled to a temperature of 20° to 23° above the boiling point of water makes maple cream. It is used as a spread on toast or English muffins. It looks something like peanut butter and spreads like peanut butter. But it tastes much, much sweeter!

34

p. 25 mold   After liquid maple candy   into small, shaped dishes where it hardens. Turned out after   shape of the dish. Maple candies come molded in fluted shapes, maple   and women, stars, and even rabbits. The shaped dishes are called molds

p. 28 reverse osmosis

      machine   Osmosis takes place when two substances are separated, the heavier one passing through a membrane. In reverse osmosis, the heavier substance is held back and the lighter one passes through. The reverse osmosis machine is a large, noisy machine that forces the sap through a filtering system. It works by electricity. The water molecules go through the filter and are flushed away. The sugar molecules are caught. About three-fourths of the water can be removed in this way.